A Spring of Dreams

By Scott Andrew Bailey

ISBN-13:
978-1512361216

ISBN-10:
1512361216

Table of Contents

Introduction

In many ways this collection was born out of frustration. I had not written a word for a few years, I had been busy getting married and starting a family as well as dealing with an increasingly stressful job. Throw into the mix losing a child and adopting another and life was getting busier and busier.

I was watching my dreams of writing fade into nothing. And in some ways I was not worried, I had new dreams to take their place.

Yet something niggled me, stories and incomplete projects prodded my conscience and dreams.

And I needed something for myself - something to deal with the stress – something that was my own as well as an outlet.

Most of all I needed to get my mind back in a creative mode.

Along came Kindle Direct Publishing. It seemed like an answer – I could polish up my completed manuscript and rather than going down the road of trying to get an agent and a publisher again I could publish direct.

I hit writer's block and apathy as well as time constraints.

I tried blogging – with the intention of writing something short each day – a journal really and making it private.

That didn't really work. I couldn't find the will to write a journal – especially when it started getting repetitive. And as it was private there was no incentive, no one to let down as it were.

Then it started to evolve all by itself. I made a few posts public and started to get social with other bloggers.

Then I started to use the blog as a way of recording and sharing our experiences along the adoption trail. This got more followers and responses. One thing I noticed was that poetry was popular among the people I was conversing with, people who seemed on my wavelength.

It should have been obvious to me all along. This was my answer. Poetry. I have always loved writing poetry and always found it easy, compared to prose. I don't claim to be any good I write purely for myself as opposed to any other writing I do where I write for an audience.

I also find it immensely therapeutic.

I just needed an incentive.

So I set myself a challenge and declared it publicly. To write a poem a day for a year. That way I could not back out.

It was the ideal solution. I could write a quick poem each day as time allowed. It could be about anything so I was not tied in anyway. It was a realistic challenge.

And it worked its wonders. It got my mind back to a place where it was dreaming again, so much so that I was quickly working on my other writing projects. I was able to complete the rewrite of my old manuscript and it flowed much easier once my mind was thinking like a poet (albeit amateur) again.

I have to confess that I did not write everyday. There were a few days when I was ill or just to busy with real life responsibilities that could not be shirked. But they were surprisingly few. Each time I dug up a poem I had written long ago and at least edited it and did some work on.

This book therefore is the culmination of that year long project. Here you will will find each poem for each day. I have edited and renamed a few as the originals were the first draft raw copies so to speak.

The originals as well as my other posts can be found at my blog at http://thehouseofbailey.wordpress.com/ under the Poetry/Poem a Day Challenge menu.

As I have said – I am not a professional poet and have not studied poetry in any way. These are just my attempts, I think they are accessible to all coming from the heart.

I hope you enjoy.

Goodnight

(Day 1 30/05/13)

Goodnight. Sleep tight. Love you with all my heart.
One snuggled cosy in bed.
One in the earth.
Mother and Father
Forever hurt.

Nation

(Day 2 32/05/13)

Kerching! Kerchang! Pow!
Our economy picks up!
Soul still desolate.

Outside the Daffodil and Pen

(Day 3 01/06/13)

I wandered lonely as a brick
That sinks and dives in stream and lake,
When all at once I was so sick,
And an awful mess I did make.
Beside the lake, beneath the trees.
Splattering my stomach in the breeze.

It must have been the bread I had
Or maybe that old Milky Way.
This puddle of sick smelt so bad
Along the margin of the bay.
Ten pints I had drunk, at a guess.
Tossing my head, I felt a mess.

The waves in my head danced, and they
Dashed my weak legs from under me.
A poet could not be so gay
As the one who stood over me.
He gazed and gazed and then in glee.
Threw up and fell down next to me.

Next morn when on my couch I lay
In vacant and in pensive mood.
I swore I'd give up drink that day.
And swore some more, it was quite rude.
But soon, once more, the cider spills.
I'll sleep again with daffodils.

Scott Andrew Bailey

Soundbox

(Day 4 02/06/13)

There are empty spaces
    left as people move on,
    of the spaces of places long gone,
of times gone by

There is a link between present and past
    an energy, a potential,
    strung between the memories gone
and the living yet to roll on

The link hums with the tension
    and the empty spaces echo back the thrum
    deep rich reverberation
layered on the past, the present, the future

Such is the music of life.

Footsteps

(Day 5 03/06/13)

Footsteps on the dusky beach
      Holes left by those gone by
        Empty

The tide turns, creeps back in
      holes become pools
        shining in the sunset

Peering beyond my reflections
      the shining water
        teems with life

Trench

(Day 6 04/06/13)

Dancing with my wife,
     last week the telegraph came:
Coughs ring round the trench

Same

(Day 7 05/06/13)

Remember this forever
For it will set you free
Listen to you mother on
How it is to be,
If you want success my child
Stay upon the path
Don't stray into the wild.

Be the same! Be the same.
All the world - loves the same.
Stand up tall, play it straight
And you'll never end up late.

With mortarboard and diploma
You'll rate with the great minds
If you become a doctor you'll win great respect
Be a great composer and get more of it yet
Don't become a poet that they will all forget
Be the same, be the same, be the same.

Be the same, be the same,
All the world - loves the same.
Tell it straight, tell it true,
No one will mess with you.

Bend the rules (when you can)
Make more profit for the man
A college education is a must I am sure
To give the frame of reference that you must endure
If you feel lost, a job is the cure!
Be the same! Be the same! Be the same

Is It Me?

(Day 8 06/06/13)

Flesh and bones and genes.
    Is that me?
Shirt and tie and jeans
    Is that me?
The places I have been.
    Is that me?
The words of praise, the blame that cuts
    Is that me?
The songs I loved, the books that I have read,
    The colours I paint, what I like in my bread.
    Are these me?

The friends I love and miss,
    That is me
The taste of beer and chat,
    That is me
The love for my wife and sons,
    That is me.
The song bursting in my lungs,
    That is me
The stories in my head
    That is me
The place where I grew up,
    where I was wed,
    where one was named, another laid to rest
That is me

Dreaming out of reach
    That is me.

Change

(Day 9 07/06/13)

Shouting into the hole that is the whole
    Nothing back.
Raging against the system that is all
    Nothing changed.
Staring at the box with the box.
    Nothing gained.
Justifying every move you make
    Not explained.

Time to change.

Scott Andrew Bailey

Red Roar

(Day 10 08/06/13)

Screaming red white and blue,
     Soaring in the clouds.
Thundering over the shore.
     Red Arrows Roar!

Normal

(Day 11 09/06/13)

The news is not normal
    We must remember that.
At home with my family, safe on the sofa.
    Working nine to five to bring home the bread
Struggling with bills but food on the table
    Enjoying friendships and family
Days out, nights in, peace, leisure, entertainment
    Warmth, safety, security and food.

Let us remember that this is our normal
    that many do not enjoy.
For them the everyday, the normal is
    hunger, poverty, murder and rape.

The news is not normal
    but we are the exception.
        What can we do in the face of desolation?

Mistress

(Day 12 10/06/13)

She is taken for granted by most
    Loved by some, hated by others.
She gives some what they want
    others are denied.
Some can't believe their luck
    Others demand too much.

She keeps alive the memory of those long gone.
    Brings music from the past
Brings together worlds apart
    Or breaks them down
Passes on words of love and hate
    Over time and space.

The famous thank her
    for everything she brings them
Other view her with jealousy
    as she gives what they cannot.
She'll save or kill her lovers
    But she is here to stay.

The Gulf

(Day 13 11/06/13)

The gulf between us grows and grows.
     I wonder were we ever close?
Is it a myth we tell ourselves?
     To give us false kudos.

One looks on one with envy
     the other with disdain
But neither can leave the contract
     for nothing is to gain?

Still the gulf grows wider
     bridges tumble down
Yet the ties are tighter
     Deeper runs the frown

Round and round this story goes
     Will it ever end
The futile fixing of a problem
     That will never end

So we have to ask ourselves
For richer? For poorer?

Carman

(Day 14 12/06/13)

I make cars
I always have
As did my father.

Prestige cars.
The most famous in the world
Made with pride.

Made with precision.
Made to last.
To shine and glide!

Every working day.
All the working hours.
My trusty hands create.

I may be steeped in habit
Tradition and old ways
But I trust in my own fate.

I support my family.
I support the plant.
And I support the land.

I pay my way my dues
while on my shoulders weighs
the burden that I support.

After all these years of toil
All the my many dues.
Imagine my surprise my boss.

I have given more than you!

Hope

(Day 15 13/06/13)

Tired and worn out so
      Going to sleep to dream of
Summer coming soon

Scott Andrew Bailey

Summer

(Day 16 14/06/13)

Bended blade of grass
Bows in the summer twilight
A warm journey home

Revision

(Day 17 15/06/13)

Swirling in the mists of history
     Mystic figures whirl
Dark silhouettes of dangerous men
     Stride along with pride

A flash of a sword, the chord of a song
     the clash of a shield, the beat of a drum.
The roar of a fire in a welcome hearth.
     The hearty sound of the comrades' laugh

The scent of a feast, the warmth of the soup.
     The strength of the beams over the hall
The smoke rising up into the straw
     All of this and still there's more

A cold wind blows, the mist rolls back,
     To show the cold hard facts

The Coal Man

(Day 18 16/06/13)

With his faithful tartan cap, its bobble flicking black dust
into the air
Holding in that tousled and already greying hair
With half hundred weight of coal to deliver down the
street
With his smiling green lorry, tiny windows at his feet
Walking up the narrow path, a smile upon his face
Care worn lines deep with dust, criss-crossed like living
lace
Bringing warmth to many homes and our own

Now the coal has gone but the lines remain beneath
silver hair
Hands hard and black with oil and years of toil and loyal
care
Has no wealth and all wealth one could want within his
soft brick walls
Always ready to respond to our lost and stranded calls
Tall as a tree and as strong against every withering
storm
A mere spanner in his hands his wonders to perform
Humble, with every reason to be mighty proud
With pride these words should be read to all aloud

On the Verge

(Day 19 17/06/13)

Broken down
Watching everyone speed by
Rushing
Hearing the gusts of wind
Smelling the broken grass
Feeling the breeze on my cheeks
Because that's all I can do while I wait

Exist

(Day 20 18/06/13)

If I
Cease to exist
Will my
heart and soul dissolve in the air?
If I
Breathe my last breath
Will my
Golden thoughts shine anywhere?
If I
unbind from this earth
And
Sail the sun
right out to the stars.
Will I
Find my way back?
Or
Roam forever that celestial park?

If I
Cease to exist
Will my
Precious dreams chase after my soul?
If I
breathe my last breath
Will my
Endless hopes continue to roll?
If I
Fly up from the earth
And
Spiral up to the bright dancing stars
Will I
Find my way back
Or
Make my home where galaxies are?

Hard to exist
Back to back to the hammer of flesh.
Gasping for breath
Tried escape from this strangling mesh.
Tied hard to the earth
Brought to ground by invisible hands.
If I
Find my way back
Will I
Find my house fallen in sands?

Shout to exist
Drink the sun and swallow the air!
Savour the breath
Turn the corner and take up the dare!
Stand firm on the earth
And
Walk the roads under the stars.
We'll find our way back
While our dreams fly where galaxies are.

Taxing

(Day 21 19/06/13)

They didn't know
Or didn't care
That corporate giants
Weren't paying their share

If they didn't know
Incompetence screams
If they didn't care
Corruption streams

Next month. Something else
To make us all forget
How many times do we take this?
Is there more give in us yet?

Sighs Matter

(Day 22 20/06/13)

Silk sliding
Fingertips brushing
Lightly

Warm breath
Close
Tingling

Lips shining
Eyes widening
Hush

Moist close
Pulsing closer
Moving

Rested Wheel

(Day 23 21/06/13)

Why aren't we railing?
Why aren't we mad?
Why do we sit in silence?
In apathy so sad.

Is the sickle blunted?
The hammer dropped and cracked?
Has the guillotine lost it's edge?
Has liberty backtracked?

The peasants have moved on
From field to factory to desk.
Is it progress beautiful
Or captivity grotesque?

So day after day
after day after day.
We struggle and toil
No time left to play.

We hand over our freedom
We hand over our cash.
While the fat cats sleep
on their growing stash.

Where is the spirit of liberty?
The hero in the square?
The lone horse trodden woman
De-fanged are those who care.

Lantern

(Day 24 22/06/13)

Old light from the past
Is still illumination
Wisdom echoes far

Tension

(Day 25 23/06/13)

Tight when I shouldn't be
Wound up in the calm
Of home and tranquillity
Lacking a balm

Lacking release
Of the spring in my neck
The wires in my heart
Keeping in check

Blessings abound
Around me and yet
Contentment's elusive
Crushed by the debt

Of responsible lives
Led slowly and sure
This then the malady
Where then the cure?

Leagues

(Day 26 24/06/13)

Today's tragedy
Is the acceptance of
Bloody league tables!

Sparks

(Day 27 25/06/13)

A sad shadow falls
Casting gloom over our dreams:
Sparks dispel the dark!

Thirteen Lines

(Day 28 26/06/13)

The bankers, the police and politicians
Laugh at us in their vaults of gold.
Shock and anger and bile!
Such arrogance we behold.

Headlines! Headlines! Headlines!
We MUST have an inquiry!
Heads must rolls, we must have scalps!
Weeks and weeks of fury.

We will not suffer injustice any longer!
Oh! there's a royal baby due.
Wait! What? Conkers have been banned!
It's health and safety gone mad!

What can you do with a shrug?

Sometimes

(Day 29 27/06/13)

Sometimes the things we are due
      do not arrive
Sometimes that precious parcel
      is lost
Sometimes the blows
      are more than we think
           we can survive
But we do

It is the ancient sadness
      of humanity
Happiness has such
      frailty

Roaming Words

(Day 30 28/06/13)

Wherever words roam
Over fantastical lands
The heart rests at home

Scott Andrew Bailey

Bricks

(Day 31 29/06/13)

Coloured bricks
Red, blue, yellow, white
And many more
Many shapes
Many sizes
No limits
Many surprises

Build a fire engine
A house, a school
A lake, a park, a city, a town
A space station and spaceships and an alien host
A castle, a bridge a knight and a ghost!

All this and more build it all
And never ever build up your wall

Spectrum

(Day 32 30/06/13)

If life were light
    shone through a prism
We would see the parts of our lives
    illuminated on the wall
From the red of our passions
    to the blue of our melancholy
And all the shades in between
    The wonderful rainbow of life

Cross

(Day 33 01/07/13)

Rapists come and go
like bills
grit your teeth
bear it
pay
Carry a dagger
close
no guarantee
a talisman
a cross

Hide in the woods
crunching leaves
above
beneath them
a thousand bones

Click, click
Bang, bang
You make it a film!
a song
a hero's theme

Click, click
Bang, bang
My mother didn't pay
didn't bear her cross
didn't carry her cross
now lays beneath hers

My best suit
stained by the passing
the violent end
of my daughter
in my arms

Now you tell me
in your yellow coat
shining stripe
proud nation
Go back whence you came!

Scott Andrew Bailey

Cross:Senryu

(Day 34 02/07/13)

Fleeing from killers
The child runs desperately
To fill out a form

Tsuma

(Day 35 03/07/13)

Silky dress caress
Swishing – lighting my desire
For your loving touch

Star Fathers (Laturne)

(Day 36 04/07/13)

Stars
Magic
Fathers dance
Under dark trees
Dream

A Lost Forest

(Day 37 05/07/13)

Bright flakes of light in dappled leaves
that float on down
where saplings grow
and settle low

And earthy scents rise in the air
As underfoot
leaves crunch and fold
red-brown and gold

The rusty fence that holds it in
it holds us too
back from that time
when we roamed free

Beach

(Day 38 06/07/13)

Beach
Crashing waves
A boy in heaven
A joyous light in his eyes
So his parent's hearts are warmed
To see his delight
Smiles on the
Beach

Balloons

(Day 39 07/07/13)

Balloons rising high
Bear kisses into the sky
Up to the lost ones

Silence

(Day 40 08/07/13)

Silence is Golden
Because it's so very rare
Grab it while you can

Pool of Dreams

(Day 41 09/07/13)

Long shadows
Cast their thoughts behind us
Dim our once bright footsteps
An unclean window screen

But flashes from sudden mirrors
Slash though the shadow forms
Glimpses of dreams that passed us
Keeping them alive

Though shadows keep on growing
We head towards the sun
In shade our dreams may swim
But they will follow until we're done

Always Descending

(Day 42 10/07/13)

Always descending, never ascending.
Moving downwards, moving down.
I can't get used to this feeling
Moving downwards, moving down.
Is it really like this? What are we doing?
Do we really want this?
Is this the thing to be?
The chains that pull the valves and the levers,
That drive the steam through pipes of dreams.

Dream worlds falling, morning calling,
Pull the chains on, shoulder the yoke.
Down to business. Down to labour.
Moving downwards, moving down.
I don't like this, what am I doing?
I don't really want this, what is to be?
Enter the shaft that takes us downwards.
The light is dimming as our dreams descend.

Walk of Knives

(Day 43 11/07/13)

Our heart leads onwards to our dreams
Our mind towards our goals
While we wend the road between
That cuts our very soles.

Today we thanked the man
Who tightened up the chains
That ties us to our solid home
For someone else's gains

If only our hearts and minds agreed
The road could be wide and straight
Let's hope we find the map we need
Before it is too late

Onshore

(Day 44 12/07/13)

What lies within that deep dark world?
That immensity of green threat
Where lies the leviathan of doom
In that swelling encompassing brine
Where plankton swirl through tentacles
That writhe and sway and curl and wave
And small fish dart discreet?
The leviathan's milky domain!
Filled with cries of beasts the creature eats
Where crescendos rise and pull the heart with sighs.
The leviathan shifts with a thrashing fit
A rumble excites the waves.
And gulls drop and chop their prey and hop
from surf to spray to cloud to rock.
The whole sea moves with a great heart's beat
Where will its great thoughts lead?
Will it be content to nibble and gnaw
Or rise with a tumultuous roar?
A great green wall with weight of stone
While here, nearby, and all alone
I
Stand
On the sand
Unsure

Caged

(Day 45 13/07/13)

Noble, graceful, caged
So like us yet so far apart
Our bars are our own

Scott Andrew Bailey

Lost Words

(Day 46 14/07/13)

Screams, shouts, whispers, words
Uttered, none heeded at all
Lost like leaves that fall

Summer Clouds

(Day 47 15/07/13)

A quivering wave
of light in light in the summer clouds
as the sun goes down

Slice of Life

(Day 48 16/07/13)

Wake up. Can't see. Sleepy eyes. Breakfast with my wife
and son.
Driving. Dropping off family. Driving to factory.
Roadworks, roadworks, roadworks
fixing a computer, picking up stock, driving, roadworks,
driving and more driving.
Work. Unloading. Testing stock, adding stock. Mortgage
questions paperwork.
Adoption paperwork missing! New firmware! Flawed.
New firmware again.
Testing testing testing. Decoding and more testing.
Problems headache, stress.
Driving home, roadworks, idiots, danger. Dinner and
playtime, fighting with son over bedtime, housework,
paperwork.
Poetry. Facebook. Paperwork, Bed time. Togetherness
and rest.

Duty

(Day 49 17/07/13)

Birds do it. Bees do it
Even the god damn fleas do it
It's in the genes to survive

It's not enough. Not for us
We have more, in our double helix
Than the ability to thrive

Make it our duty
Transcend circumstance!

Runs Through Trees

(Day 50 18/07/13)

Slowly shifting canopy
Layer on layer soft light green
Waving like courtesan fans
Sun winking through

Seedlings drifting down sunbeams
Dappled brown leafy ground
Scent of earth
Rough feel of bark

Through this I run!
And the forest's essence
Enters my senses
Vitalises my blood!

Dreams in the Universe

(Day 51 19/07/13)

Motes of dust
So we have been described
Floating in the vastness of time and space
Small, inconsequential
Dust motes made of dust from ancient dead stars
Yet
So far
Amongst all we see
the star fields of diamond dust,
the ancient piercing light,
the glowing, magical, wispy nebulae,
the rainbow rings of Saturn,
the storms of Jupiter,
the blinding light of supernova,
the singular dark of a black hole,
world after world
galaxy after galaxy
Nowhere have we found
Yet
Anything that compares
to the complexity, the wonder, the intricacy,
the magic
of
the thoughts of you and I

There Yet

(Day 52 20/07/13)

I am almost there
At the point of completion
Forever it seems

Silver Icons

(Day 53 21/07/13)

Shining argent in sunlight or silver sheen in the rain
Letter, rings, lions. Phoenix or tiny names
Even flying angels and leaping fluid cats
Bright, alluring but for many
The last thing they will see

Purple Star

(Day 54 22/07/13)

Deep bright purple star
Piercing from the depths of roiling blue gas clouds
And a million billion stars
Outshining Venus and Mars
Swathes like silver paths
Some gathered in spiral wheels
And between them in the sparse dark spaces
Ships blink and travel on by
A memory from the deepest well of childhood
A memory that could not have been

Green Fingers

(Day 55 23/07/13)

Green fingers
Rip open the rusty shell
Slow tendrils with irresistible grasp
Dealt with by a blade or chemical wash
They will be back
In time victory will be theirs

The World in A Book

(Day 56 24/07/13)

The world in a book
For my son
To show him the places
Across the seas
That he dreams of
The colours
The creatures
The cultures and the clashes
The world in a book in his hands
As one day
The world will be in his hands

The Man in The Tree

(Day 57 25/07/13)

The man in the tree
The plank
The turned leg
The joint
The dust and the shavings

The tree in the man
The setting down of deep roots
The reaching for the skies
The drinking deep of the earth
The steadfastness and the wielding

Class of Blood

(Day 58 26/07/13)

You people
Little people
You don't understand.
It's tradition
It's sport
It's in our genes
Our mixed up genes
Blood
Jobs are created
By the sport we choose
By the blood we shed
Surely that's enough
Of course
The same can't be said
For you
And your cock fights

Tree

(Day 59 27/07/13)

Two trees
Old as memory
Some leaves fallen
A root cut off
Two trees
Explored
Examined
Noted down
Two trees drawn together
Forever entwined

Scott Andrew Bailey

Winter Ice

(Day 60 28/07/13)

Nothing, nothing, blank
Beneath winter's hard black ice
Water flows freely

The New

(Day 61 29/07/13)

The new can't replace the should have been
The should have been haunts us forever
Though the new will be a healer
And receive all our love just the same
It's pointless being angry at fate
But that doesn't stop the burn
The frisson on top of everyday stress
For the should have been we always yearn.
The new will have their own should have been
So maybe we will understand
And make a happier will be
At least that is the plan

The Conduit

(Day 62 30/07/13)

A conduit, a bridge or a gateway
It goes under many old names
Open it with wonder and reverence
For the spell will then be under-way

The weakest of hands can undo it
The portal of magical ways
Connecting one mind to another
With a delicate ethereal wave

Some portals are heavy and dusty
Some dance with electrical sparks
But they all do the same, all show the way
For strange dreams from heart to heart

There were even once living gateways
Who opened the way with a look
Always there's one right beside us
The conduit, the gateway, the book

Cold Cold News

(Day 63 31/07/13)

The news chills today
The child killers found guilty
Will justice suffice?

Energy

(Day 64 01/08/13)

Starlight is silent
Waves crash and roar on the shore
Then there is matter

Traffic (Tanka)

(Day 65 02/08/13)

Brushed by death today
Twice. Metal boxes speeding
Too fast, too near me
Driven on by the wrong thoughts
Or expensive wanderings

Scott Andrew Bailey

Raw

(Day 66 03/08/13)

More than a year's passed
Memory is still red raw
Watching blue eyes fade

Ancient Coast

(Day 67 04/08/13)

Where the crashing sea
Meets the shifting, cracking ice
Hunters hunker down

Scott Andrew Bailey

Time Cycle

(Day 68 05/08/13)

Time and time again
So it is out with the new
In with the older

Through the Glass (Villanelle)

(Day 69 06/08/13)

Slowly the shadows pass
As memories retreat and fade
Passing beyond the glass

Like springtime budding grass
New joys together are made
Slowly the shadows pass

This pain we will surpass
And sunbeams will cascade
Passing beyond the glass

Though sometimes the shattered glass
Will cut us like a blade
Slowly the shadows pass

New light will surely trespass
On the lawn that we have made
Passing beyond the glass

Those memories we can't bypass
But their colour has finally greyed
Slowly the shadows pass
Passing beyond the glass

The Show

(Day 70 07/08/13)

Bug me, drug me
    You'll never touch my mind
Not that you want to
    Afraid of what you'll find

Afraid of the secrets
    Of someone in the know
Afraid of the exposure
    Of your elaborate show

So go on with your programme
    Sticking to the script
Until the day you are aware
    You're playing in a crypt

The Songbird

(Day 71 08/08/12)

Bird sings by the pool
in the spring in a soft cool breeze
her voice a sweet sound

Scott Andrew Bailey

Autumn

(Day 72 09/08/13)

Autumn golden brown
covers the hard icy ground
a leafy carpet

So It Goes

(Day 73 10/08/13)

Stereotypical headlines
    Reactions just the same
Ample opportunity
    To apportion blame

Night time is for thinking
    Sorting truth from lies
But in the sunshine morn
    Dreams just fly

The Cracked Vase

(Day 74 11/08/13)

The vessel is cracked
Still holds the sacred blooms
Still revered
Though the blooms are without root
Rootless. Dying.

Still revered
Water though refreshed
Still stagnates
Dead blooms replaced
With freshly cut.

Repetition
Builds a patina of respect
Authority
Habit.

The vessel is cracked
Empty of life
Yet forever filled
and revered.

Flown

(Day 75 12/08/13)

Another one lost
Too short, too precious, and gone
Little heart flown high

Green Board

(Day 76 13/08/13)

Turn upon turn upon turn upon turn
Green upon green upon green upon green
Tracks and tracks and shining silver
Decision making machine

Can it take the pressures
Of expectations on board?
Will I?

Modern Times

(Day 77 14/08/13)

Primary colours or simple fruit
Clickety click click and point
Open the way to a blind deluge
Illuminate the mind

Bright blinding highway – super-fast
On a never-ending roll
Swallow it all until we drown
Where is the straw of truth?

Burton (Clerihew)

(Day 78 15/08/13)

Sir Richard Francis Burton
For who life was so certain
He was a master of disguise
Caught Mecca by surprise

Dream Bearer

(Day 79 16/08/13)

The bearer of news is coming
The bearer of mystery
Will the news be good
Or scary

The bearer of news is coming
Anticipation is strong
Slowly our dreams are condensing
So long, so long, so long.

Scott Andrew Bailey

Wonder Shore

(Day 80 17/08/13)

Back from the shore
Into my arms
After an explore
In a world of charms

A world full of wonder
Mystery and fun
Of beaches and crabs
And space to run

Breathe salty air
Hear laughter ring
Dance without a care
What tomorrow may bring

So dance more my son
Enjoy sun and sea
When the day is done
Run back home to me

Poor Race

(Day 81 18/08/13)

As a race
We should step up
To eliminate the gap
Between the haves and the have-nots
Between the singers with their bling and the slaves on
the line
Between the bankers with their blank cheques and the
children in poverty
For most of history most men women and children
Lived in misery, died hungry.
We are a disgrace
As a race

Society

(Day 82 19/08/13)

Is society
Tension on the webs between
Elites and masses

In Sickness and Hope

(Day 83 20/08/13)

Tiredness saps me
Nausea weakens my soul
Hope is a hand up

Open Gate

(Day 84 21/08/13)

So the gate opens
Let's see where the road will go
As I bare my soul

Who's the Fool

(Day 85 22/08/13)

Listen to all the anger
Hark at all the fury
Just remember that
You no longer own the jury

Humiliate the whistleblower
Make him out a fool
Wielding propaganda
Like an old blunt tool

Don't you know we're cynics now
We can see through all the lies
You will have to do much better
Or suffer the surprise

Intolerance

(Day 86 23/08/13)

I am a tolerant man no more

Intolerant of inequality
    And all who promote it
Intolerant of injustice
    And all those who peddle it
Time to make the world
    The way it should be

Pain in the Back

(Day 87 24/08/13)

A pain in the back
Plus lack of sleep is the bane
Of relaxation

Scott Andrew Bailey

Evening Beach

(Day 88 25/08/13)

Splashing on the beach
Throwing pebbles in the surf
With red sun sinking

Winter's Wind

(Day 89 26/08/13)

Winter's wind blows fierce
through silk and wood it does pierce
a lonely howling

Scott Andrew Bailey

Sonnet for our Times

(Day 90 27/08/13)

So it seems to me that beyond the news
Beyond the web of the media spin
There are places still where the only views
Are battlegrounds full of unearthly din

I see the most pious places burning
Where the holy words still hold high accord
Where simple souls for peace are still yearning
The peace that those holy words won't afford

Yet here where reason and science abound
We live comfy lives secure in our ways
No bombs rain down on our manicured ground
There is no revolt, no passion ablaze

There's something wrong with this picture I see
Is it really this way, can you tell me?

Memory Lane

(Day 91 28/08/13)

Sound, sound, drumbeat hard
Too loud, who cares, light flashing
Thumping beat, hot air, alcohol haze
Saturday nights of days gone by

Boxy

(Day 92 29/08/13)

Worn out, knackered, done
A brimful of boxy fun
In old Legoland

Fallout

(Day 93 30/08/13)

Taut relationship
Strained over a bloody mess
Chemical fallout

Web

(Day 94 31/08/13)

Glistening silver
A delicate spider web
Fallen tree around

Debt

(Day 95 01/09/13)

Do not lightly discard them
with tales of the foolish bold.
They sat for weeks, for months, for years
in trenches freezing cold.
Sometimes feet simply mouldered
in the sucking mud.
And now and then they'd rise and run
and spill their loyal blood.

Do not belittle the suffering
of soldiers now long dead.
With nothing but talk and songs and bombs
bursting in their head.
Bound together with chains of love
shattered by leaden death.
They ended as they had begun
with cries upon their breath.

Do not lightly remember them
with only paper flowers.
They faced the fear, the pain, the cold,
for hours and hours and hours.
They ran together and fell alone
upon those foreign fields.
Protecting those they loved
those frightened human shields.

Do not read these words and think
that these things are past.
Do not think you will not hear
that deep and dreadful blast.
Do not sit in decadence
and take for granted peace.
You owe a debt to those who died
and that debt will never cease.

Shadows

(Day 96 02/09/13)

Our voices are simply the shadows
Cast by our dreams and thought
If the shadows become ineffectual
Then our voices will end up as naught
Yet shadows can give us the outline
Of what is looming above
If we take note of the darkness
We can give those dreams a shove
One thing we must yet remember
To give those shadows a shape
Sunlight is needed behind it
From brightness the dreams will escape

Walls

(Day 97 03/09/13)

Yet another wall
How many before we're home?
Prevaricating

Divine

(Day 98 04/08/13)

Imagine
Me
I kill without discrimination
for race, for age, for sex or sexuality
I take saints and sinners
I take your loved ones
in return
I deal you pain
without explanation
when asked
the answer is
that you cannot hope to understand me
As a man
you would lock me up
revile me
or label me insane
But I am divine
So that's OK then

Steely Stress

(Day 99 05/09/13)

The lights on the corners of the boxes of steel
Are giving me a pain in the head
Like the fools who drive slowly in the outside lane
They are driving but their brains are dead

They have a purpose those lights you see
And I expect them to flash
Maybe that is my big mistake
Forgetting people are so rash

Reality

(Day 100 06/09/13)

No reality
That's what attracts them
No history, no baggage
Only dreams of the night
That's the attraction of the mistresses,
the hookers and the one night stands
No reality

Better to live in real love
Than empty dreams

Twines

(Day 101 07/09/13)

Silver twines
intricate wires
thin and delicate
stretching from misty past
to infinite future
Each one a story
a thread of life
Twisting they come together
Winding, entwining
Further down the road
The twines form a rope
Stronger
Older
Wiser
Thicker
Stiffer

The Joke

(Day 102 08/09/13)

I am a mirror
Distorted
Even cracked
But a reflection still
I share with you my fear
And passion
My fear is blue
Deep dark blue
All sharp angles
Like shark fins
And knives
Fear that turns me
As white as a clown
Alas, my fear is my passion
My love
I seek it out
To taste the thrill
Of the fear and the chase
And I share it out
While I play my games
With the orphan
The fear
The dark, dark blue
That bears
The sign of the bat

Ancient Wanderers

(Day 103 09/09/13)

Wandering the shore
Through new lands everyday
Ancient fishermen

Storms

(Day 104 10/09/13)

Clouds piling up dark
Lightning flashing – sky to ground
Rumbling all around

Two Years

(Day 105 11/09/13)

Pardon me for interrupting
But that was just a step too far
Not really a sporting move
Two years
Two years you have been playing straight
That is to say
Murdering
But with the proper tools
The ones from our markets
Hardware, hard and solid and paid for
That gas – tut tut – just too far
So hand it over
There's a good chap
And we will let you
Get back to your war

Scott Andrew Bailey

Proud Dad

(Day 106 12/09/13)

Hushed concentration
Then with a sudden surprise
His name is written!

Late

(Day 107 13/09/13)

Eleven fifty
Nine and almost out of time
Yet still ploughing on

The Pool

(Day 108 14/09/13)

They trickle in
The protesters, the bitter, the dispossessed, the poor
They swirl in slow currents
Exchanging thoughts, views, ideas.
An oasis for the outcasts

The Man sits by the pool
And fishes
Taking what he needs
Watching the rest

The pool holds no threat

Twentieth Century Taliesin

(Day 109 15/09/13)

I am the factory wall, despised and so defaced
Covered with graffiti, defiled and disgraced.
I am the concrete tower that holds up the concrete road
Bleak and faceless white, bearing my toxic load.
I am the bin on the street, bursting full with waste
Where rats and vermin crawl, around me in distaste.
I am the battered traffic cone abandoned in the hedge
A used forgotten prize of lives lived on the edge.
I am the street side gutter where dirty water flows
A place of infestation, where all the darkness goes.
I am the discarded knife with bloodstains on the blade
The close but unseen menace lurking in the shade.
I am the lofty tower spewing clouds into the air
That speed across the oceans, killing without a care.
I am the broken shelf with screws rent from the wall
That supported all the books and caused them all to fall.
I am the sodden cardboard box flapping in the street
Broken, limp, forgotten, always under feet.

Once I was a poet, bright browed with golden hair
Playing harp and singing, songs into the air.
Once I was a druid learning from the trees
Drawing strength from bark and wisdom from the
leaves.
Once I was a warrior with proud and shining sword
Singing with my warband a deep heroic chord.
Once I was a chieftain with princes round my hearth
Against war and cold and famine our mighty hearts did
laugh.
Once I was a king whose soul was all the land
Who tended all his people with a strong and generous
hand.

But I made other people suffer
Now suffer myself in turn.
But as you wreak your vengeance
What lesson do you learn?

What lessons do you all forget?

Gathering Clouds

(Day 110 16/09/13)

Dark gathering clouds
Brooding and beautiful
Waiting for the flash of light
The spark
The piercing blue white crack
And the wind
The raw whipping wind
And the release of rain
and the rainbow

Repeating Lives

(Day 111 17/09/13)

Taking my son to my old school
Following the bus I used to take
Still the same number
Basically the same model
The same smell of classrooms
And I wonder
Is this it?
Are we destined
To repeat lives?

It is not enough
I want more
More for my children
Than was there for me
No fear
More doors
No prejudice
More joy
In knowledge

Is that too much to ask?

News

(Day 112 18/09/13)

What's behind the story
What is the reason for that news
Who gets the benefit, the prize
The envelope with the bread
The law successfully passed
The company track greased
Somebody's life made easier
At the cost of somebody else

Errors

(Day 113 19/09/13)

Mistakes seep into
Our minds through repetition
Habitual truth's born

Uncaring Mirth

(Day 114 20/09/13)

Laughter echoes
In rarefied halls
Between clinks from glasses
Raised in champagne toasts
While expensive soles
Walk heavy
On broken dreams and despair

Nostalgia

(Day 115 21/09/13)

Worn wooden floor
Distant, ancient scent
Tobacco long gone
Beer, deep red in thick glass
Salt and vinegar crisps
Pickled eggs
Pickled patrons
Warmth and welcome
Long gone like the smoke
One missed

The House of Bailey

(Day 116 22/09/13)

Heart lifts
When I lift him high
Heart skips
With her every kiss
Through darkness and troubled times
Our place has held us
I return with joy
To the walls
My son
My wife
My home

Galaxy (A Nonet)

(Day 117 23/09/13)

Swirling, whirling milky clouds of stars
Spiralling down to the black hole
Supermassive hungry dark
Swallowing all it can
Axle of the wheel
Sparkling star arms
Shining cloud
Holds our
Home

Wandering Spells

(Day 118 24/09/13)

Is it enough?
These words
We gather here
From across the globe
Our thoughts thrumming
Over strands of the web
They gather and agree
Mostly
And we know
What is wrong with the world
What is right
How to behave
And with well picked words
We condemn
Or cajole
the effective ones.
But is it enough?
Just the words.

Yet once upon a time
There was a spell
A magical combination
That set me on this course
Of reason and reason-ability

Maybe it is enough
If someone somewhere
Is moved by our spells
To do the right thing.

Chipping Away at Mountains

(Day 119 25/09/13)

Lines and words and lines
On one screen they mean this
Elsewhere something else
On paper strangely old
Before my eyes
Flashing by
Doing magic
But why
For the small ends
Of small goals
Chipping away at mountains

Hatchets

(Day 120 26/09/13)

Porcelain tiles
Cold on my cheek
How did I get here?
When did I fall asleep?

The hatchet in my head
Overpowers the hatchet in my heart
For now
And then it begins again

Golden liquid calls

Sensitive

(Day 121 27/09/13)

My eyes are sensitive to the light
They are filtered
Protected by shades
What about my heart?
My feelings?

No filter please
I am sensitive
I need all the light let in.

Sold

(Day 122 28/09/13)

We can make you a better parent
Just come and bank with us
We can make you a better lover
Just use our scent
We can make you more successful
Just drive our cars
We can make you a better man
Just drink our beers
We can make you young and cool
Just use our phones
We can make you healthier
Just eat our food

Give us your money
So we can fill the gaps
Of your so obviously
Empty lives

Fragile

(Day 123 29/09/13)

So many connections
So many lines
All taut and humming
Junctions and switches
A house of cards
Delicately balanced
Systems
Working to full capacity
One break from collapse
Such is life

Rising Tide

(Day 124 30/09/13)

From the shallows to the icy deep
Where dolphins dance and starfish sleep
Through swaying kale and shifting sand
Feel the touch of an oily hand

Where lights speed by in total dark
Where rest many a sunken ark
Where through the kale fish do slip
Feel a cold and choking grip

Where bubbles rise and currents surge
Where waters from the heavens merge
Where weight does crush both bones and rock
Feel the iron fingers lock

And here my heart it swells and roars
From roiling dark to shattered shores
And I will rise with fury's might
And crush the hand that picks this fight

So fear the shark with jaws that rend
And the mighty swell that shall bend
Every fence and dam and wall
And drown the rumble of cliffs that fall

And when the hand has done its deed
You will curse your dirty seed
And then at last you will see
How small you are beside the sea

Prevailing

(Day 125 01/10/13)

Lost to us, never forgotten
Unusual tides took him away
Carried to peace and to sleep
And even as the dark will swell
Sad, but sad will not prevail

The List That Should Not Have Been

(Day 126 02/10/13)

Tragic stories
Behind smiling faces
And pleading eyes
How did it come to this

Wallowing

(Day 127 03/10/13)

Corrupt. Wealthy. Safe.
Wallowing in filthy loot
And laughing at us

Health Gains

(Day 128 04/10/13)

Giving people health
Appears low priority
Set against profits

Consumed

(Day 129 05/10/13)

More fucking shopping
I'm consumed by consuming
Working just keeps up

Formation

(Day 130 06/10/13)

A single mote
of stardust
sparkles bright
in endless black
drifting
No goal,
no direction
for time
that feels
eternity
Nothing
Cold, cold
Nothing
And then
Attracted to another
Bright shining mote
Joined together
Bound in twisting dance
round and round
and down
What seems forever
togetherness
never apart
again

The other comes
with more attachments
gathering around
A family, a clan
a get together that has no end
a bouncy, rowdy party
as things heat up

And the happening attracts more
and the numbers swell
the dances speed and the steps
multiply with complexity
The place is hotting up
as events coalesce

Then the point of no return
This is the place to be
the single mote has pulled
more that could be dreamed
and the crowds rush in and in
and down
the crowds become a crush
And the heat gives rise to new forms of dance
and new energy as the crowds arise

And then the circle is complete
as the fire starts to burn and the lonely mote
is now the heart
of brand new burning star

Relief

(Day 131 07/10/13)

Weight from shoulders lifts
Unanimous approval
The road is still long

Ups and Downs

(Day 132 08/10/13)

From joy to worry
As sickness strikes yet again
Families hold tight

Cable Ties

(Day 133 09/10/13)

Cables tie us
Hold us tight
To one spot
Even invisible ones
Chains
Keeping us busy
Keeping us attentive
Keeping us productive
and consuming
So when they are cut
We are lost
Unable to produce
As we once did

Scott Andrew Bailey

The Dark

(Day 134 10/10/13)

The darkness where the heart beats fast
The shadows where no moonlight's cast
The deepest dell of starless nights
Gleaming eyes the only light

The sound of cold and ancient breath
On the breeze the scent of death
A rustle from behind the trees
A snapping twig the blood to freeze

The conflict of the fright or flight
But where to run on icy night?
The frozen legs the burning fear
The certainty of danger near

Imagination births these fears
But even as the presence nears
Pointing out what we must mark
Why do we so fear the dark

Night Forest

(Day 135 11/10/13)

A silver sylph slips silent through the trees
Spreading silver stardust upon the trees
Disappearing into the deep shadows
Where foxes hunt

Blunt Hammer

(Day 136 12/10/13)

When horror is turned to love
And death has become high romance
Do the forces of the underworld
Practice a jubilant dance

Do vampires laugh with glee
And werewolves lick their fangs
As they open up their gates
With fanfares, bells and clangs

And into their arms they run
The poorly misguided youth
And their heroes welcome them in
With claw and jaw and tooth

Time Slips

(Day 137 13/10/13)

Our most precious coin
Swamped by trivial demands
Yet can't be ignored

Brain Dead

(Day 138 14/10/13)

Brain dead tonight
Can't think straight
Waiting for the muse
To open my mind's gate

Candles

(Day 139 15/10/13)

One lumen
The light of a candle
It can be seen they say
For many miles
Candles burn tonight
One for each lost angel
Light that will been seen over many years
Still bright in our minds
A million candles
A fiery sun of bittersweet memories
The burning potential
Of lives that never were

Deep Red

(Day 140 16/10/13)

Deep red-brown
Liquid
Augmented by amber light
White top
Gold badge
Warmth
And slow appreciation

Bound to Serve

(Day 141 17/10/13)

Bound to serve
The master that we crave
Enduring the pain
Not struggling in the ties
That bind
Taking the punishment
Utter submission
Belittled
Stripped
Of dignity
All for the reward
The release
The coin

Sick

(Day 142 18/10/13)

Feel as sick as a dog
Too much work not enough play
Dulling the senses

Winding Words

(Day 143 19/10/13)

Master of words
By words mastered
Many a politician can claim
Those that abuse the power
By which they rose
Will be bitten by the beast they tamed

Such is the reality
We choose to believe
But the truth we know is worse
Where corruption rules
It protects its own
Mostly, the corrupt rule

Drained

(Day 144 20/10/13)

Every buzz and chime
On the phone
Is a worry
Something has gone down
Something is wrong
Another demand
On my time and my brain
Which are both drained
Something
Must change

Seven Years

(Day 145 21/10/13)

Seven years
They say it's wool
Well I have my little lamb
To keep me warm
And hope to hold her
Beyond diamond!

Scott Andrew Bailey

Sustenance

(Day 146 22/10/13)

Cheese, onions, bread and beer
Like it or hate it
Sharing an experience
Over thousands of years

I/O

(Day 147 23/10/13)

The information superhighway
It is a heavy weight
Data, redundancy
Processes
Alerts
Objectification
Frames
Presentations and investors
Response
Time
High availability
Validity
Technical, radical, practical, logical
Balancing load
Stresses
Testing
Testing
Test

Craving
Simplicity

Man

(Day 148 24/10/13)

I am the hunter
The bringer down of prey
The destroyer
The shadow
The bringer of fear.
I am the master of war
The hoarder of riches
The steel lord
The holder of lightning
I am strength and glory

So why do I still struggle in vain

The King

(Day 149 25/10/13)

The King who was
And shall be
Stirs restive in his sleep
Sword in hand
Ready
Who will it smite?
Invaders or haters
Will justice by the sword
Ever be served?

Scott Andrew Bailey

Epic

(Day 150 26/10/13)

He slew the great beast
Whose mother took her revenge
The great Beowulf

Party

(Day 151 27/10/13)

Passing the parcel
Noisy musical statues
Children's birthday joy

Poppies

(Day 152 28/10/13)

Time for the flowers to bloom again
Red
Like blood
That was shed
A century ago
And every day since
One day
They will be white

Dreaming

(Day 153 29/10/13)

Tiny starbursts
The peak on tiny waves
Deep green over yellow
Swaying weeds
Dappled stones
Dark fish darting
The scent of rich water
And reeds
Time to watch
Relax
The life I crave
Instead
Work, bills, sleep, stress

Scott Andrew Bailey

To The Bone

(Day 154 30/10/13)

A pounding headache
The fruit of today's labour
Now going to sleep

Demons

(Day 155 31/10/13)

Trick or treating
With our son
For the first time
Wishing the other
Were here
As the demons cavort
and dance
Gathering their loot
Doing their worst
Other flesh freezes
Starved of food and hope
Is one man's fun
Another's murder?

Water

(Day 156 01/11/13)

A silent sunset
Calm waters ripple slowly
Dark storm clouds gather

Fireworks (Triolet)

(Day 157 02/11/13)

Hand in hand we all walk tonight
Mother, Father and loving son
Watching darkness bursting with light
Hand in hand we all walk tonight
Sky flowers blooming burn our sight
This time of year is always fun
Hand in hand we all walk tonight
Mother, Father and loving son

Sparrow

(Day 158 03/11/13)

Sparrow, sparrow in my way.
Briefly tell your tale today.
Tell me if my love is dead.
Do I waste the tears I shed?

Briefly now I'll tell my tale.
Pray your courage does not fail.
You do not waste the tears you shed.
Alas I say, your love is dead.

A sharp, cold sword did spill her blood.
She tried to stem an angry flood.
But peace that day she could not win.
So fearful war will begin.

Thank you bird for being true.
Nothing's left for me to do.
To take up arms and pursue strife.
Slay the spoilers of my life.

I bid you sir, think awhile.
Turn from this dark path so vile.
Listen to my humble song.
Step not where your lover's gone.

Just a simple bird am I
But far above this land I fly.
And see its beauty spread below.
See ahead, where you might go.

Lay down your sword with forgiving heart.
Do not tear your land apart.
Still your rage and vengeance cease.
Follow rather a path of peace.

Humble bird I hear your song.
But my love is dead and gone.
So I raise my sword today.
And will make those killers pay.

The enemies that broke my heart.
And now have torn the land apart.
Upon their heads is all this blood.
For I must release the flood.

Then sir, I shall shed a tear.
For the future I do not fear.
Yet for now I swiftly go.
To make way for the crow.

Around and Around

(Day 159 04/11/13)

Electron around and around an atom's core
Atoms around and around each other
Mass around mass and air around rock
Rock around and around rock
Moon around and around earth
Earth around and around Sun
A billion suns around galactic core
Spiralling into the dark
A billion galaxies dance their endless dance
Around and around and around

I stand still

Highlands

(Day 160 05/11/13)

Tarns tributaries tumble down
heather cloaked hills
red-brown tufts twitching in the wind
Cold water, cold air, eagle riding the high winds
Wolves range over moors
Sheep shiver, shepherds huddle
Fire crackles, broth steams
Tarns tributaries tumble down
heather cloaked hills

Time is Up

(Day 161 06/11/13)

The fat white man
Built a castle
And ruled within his walls
Lived with impunity
and flowing wealth
A harem for his use
and other toys
spiced and prepared
He slumps
In his foetid
white
flesh
Those without
devalued
cheap
Turned cheapness to gold
Built better
Bigger castle

The fat white man
Never noticed the decline
The decaying walls
The deserters
The fall

Time
is
Up

Dive

(Day 162 07/11/13)

There was a young diver called laurel
Who spent her life in the coral
Of the men of the land
She dismissed them offhand
As she found them just far too amoral

Snoring

(Day 163 08/11/13)

Snoring on my chest
Warmth and love resting at peace
An early night in

Word Journey

(Day 164 09/11/13)

Clang, chip! clang chip! Clang chip! Blow.
Scratch, dip. Scratch, dip. Scratch, dip. Flow.
Block, press. Block press. Block, press. Squeeze.
Click, roll. Click, roll. Click, roll. Please.
Clackety clack. Clackety clack. Clackety clack. Slide.
Tip tap tap. Tip tap tap. Tip tap tap. Pride.
Stone to scroll to press to type to screen.
Where next the word?

Eyes (Septolet)

(Day 165 10/11/13)

Eyes
Red and raw
Seen too much

Filled
With work
and bills
and tears

Red Petals

(Day 166 11/11/13)

Red
Swathes in fields
Too many

Black and white
The headlines
That sowed the seed

Grey
The problems
The ethics
The guns

Yellow
the gas
and the memories

Red
Remembrance
and ledger

Tuesday Blue

(Day 167 12/11/13)

Crisis everyday
When did this start?
When will normality
Return
Is this the price
Of years of hard work
Maybe I should just sweep roads
Noble simplicity

Glory Days

(Day 168 13/11/13)

So the soldier walks alone
beneath the
starry night
He has no aim but distance
from the bloody fight
But the war it still pursues him
snapping at his heels
He slips into the forest deep
beyond those broken hills

O glory days
Those glory days
They've shattered
and they fade
They only left a rumour
A shadow
where they laid

So the sword is silenced
with a deep and lasting chill
In his heart the war goes on
the beating never still
Behind the hallowed orders
that laid so many low
Is revealed the empty truth
the sickest, cruellest blow

O glory days
Those glory days
They're gone
they never were
So the soldier walks away
from guilt
that he defers

Scott Andrew Bailey

Blue Star

(Day 169 14/11/13)

Blue star beam
Slides by a smoky moon
Dances through Saturn's rings
A lone abyssal tune
Lingers by the Jovian storms
Then on to lunar dust
Down through cool and silent sky
Drawn down and down like lust
Brief it touches silken skin
Pauses for a spell
Then down into the darkness
Of the iris that does swell.

Who

(Day 170 15/11/13)

Flames flicker
Time ticks
Down
War draws
Nearer
For the quick
End of time
Draws near
Who will heal
The rifts?

Alcyone (Pleiades)

(Day 171 16/11/13)

Another spirit lost
Awash in the swell and foam
Anguished over lost love
Anger dealt him the blow
Arising from the sea
Alighting on the air
A bright bird arises

Asterope (Pleiades)

(Day 172 17/11/13)

A nymph darts between trees
Afraid of the hunter
Always close behind her
Away she flees in haste
Another danger lurks
At her feet as she runs
A butterfly is born

Calaeno (Pleiades)

(Day 173 18/11/13)

Caressed by the wide sea
Corals catch the new child
Carry her to the shore
Colliding with bright fate
Climbing into the sky
Coronal light shines out
Cascading to the sea

Electra (Pleiades)

(Day 174 19/11/13)

Ever shining bright spark
Equalizing her rage
Encompassing justice
Ever seeking revenge
Endless pain unanswered
Echoing from murder
Electra takes her aim

Maia (Pleiades)

(Day 175 20/11/13)

Mother of he who brought
Music up to the Gods
Malice turned to justice
Magic cascading from
Mother of the world storm
Mighty God of the earth
Must meet a mortal end

Archibald the Wizard

(Day 176 21/11/13)

Archibald the Wizard
Is a very dodgy man.
He seeks out naughty snowstorms
And sends them to Japan.

He'd like to paint Picasso
Or Cézanne if he could.
He sends up purple smoke signs
From a tower in the wood.

He strums a harp a little
And bangs an old tin can.
Has Beaujolais on chips
According to the plan.

He strikes an unheard chord
In the hearts of all he sees.
But still he sends those snowflakes
Over oriental Seas.

Cross him at your peril
As many have found out.
Beneath his smoking jacket
Lies a sherry lout.

He doesn't care for you or me
He doesn't care at all.
He plots and schemes and gurgles.
Behind his wobbly wall.

Tear

(Day 177 22/11/13)

Is it too late for
Tears and grief to rise again
I can't hold them back

Merope (Pleiades)

(Day 178 23/11/13)

Marriage was forbidden
Mortal husband taken
Masked in a veil of shame
Must watch her husband's pain
Most faint in the heavens
Marred by following love
Misty those lives above

Taygete (Pleiades)

(Day 179 24/11/13)

The hunter is hunted
Twisting between the trees
Turned into doe from nymph
Trailed by her lover's bow
Tumbling through the forest
Two golden horns that shine
To rise into the skies

Seven Sisters

(Day 180 24/11/13)

Seven sisters done
Their stories written down now
Still their light shines on

Scott Andrew Bailey

Pounding

(Day 181 26/11/13)

My heart is racing
Not for love but for madness
It is pounding fast

Ring of Justice (Kyrielle)

(Day 182 27/11/13)

In golden age where steel was king
Rich voices of great bards there ring
The rising pride of knights there swells
Around the ring where justice dwells

Behind the throne where power lies
The dark intent deep in his eyes
The ancient druid gathers spells
Around the ring where justice dwells

The jealous son holds his dark ire
Until it rises to a fire
Bells of doom ring their deathly knells
Around the ring where justice dwells

And so the cracks came from within
Mens' convictions so very thin
Shattered by those doom laden bells
Around the ring where justice dwells

Surf

(Day 183 28/11/13)

Reverberating
Boom! Surf crashes on the shore
Golden sand twinkles

Stress

(Day 184 29/11/13)

Supposed to relax
From the endless stress of work
The phone doesn't stop

Scott Andrew Bailey

Squares

(Day 185 30/11/13)

Squares in squares
for squares like us
Or little robots
Or shining fruit
Or a myriad of penguins
Take your choice

Indoor Explorers
(A Florette)

(Day 186 01/12/13)

We brave explorers together
Wearing imitation leather
And as silent as a feather
We toiled through the darkest weather onto our prize

Through mountains and valleys we walked
By tigers and lions were stalked
And as brave as we always talked
There came a time when we just baulked against the size

Of the hunger in our bellies
Off with our explorer wellies
Broke out the ice cream and jellies
And retreated to the telly's noisy comfort

Dark

(Day 187 02/12/13)

We create darkness
Where we can't explain
Powerful darkness
Dark Matter
Holds the universe together
Dark Energy
Expands it fast
But most powerful of all
Dark Ignorance
This will tear us apart

Sound of

(Day 188 03/12/13)

So we worry like old men
On the road to night again
Wondering what the dawn will bring
Will we hear the lonely blackbird sing
And then the heart beats a skip once more
As our dreams falter

Complex systems crowd our minds
Light penetrating through the blinds
Nowhere safe to settle down our thoughts
No reprise to high ethereal courts
And so we close our eyes to the blinding light
and slowly we falter

Solid waters chills our bones
Sitting in the orange cones
Going nowhere on this winding road
Never understanding the blinking code
So we ride on ignorance and bliss
and never alter

Little Pill

(Day 189 04/12/13)

Exhaustion seeps in
Draining away all my will
Where's my little pill

Trying (Tyburn)

(Day 190 05/12/13)

Sighing
Trying
Flying
Buying
Here am I just Sighing, Trying hard
To start of my Flying, Buying time

Until One Day

(Day 191 06/12/13)

Two
Ribbons
Of mist
Hang
Twirling slowly
Around him
Sitting
Silent
In his cage
A cage of
Gold chains
And
Silver bars
Built of responsibility
Parenthood
Husbandhood
Manhood
The cage compresses
The darkness that
Fills it
Darkness surrounds him
Tries to engulf him
But the ribbons of mist
Twirl
Slowly
As he waits
Until One Day

Seeking

(Day 192 07/12/13)

Swimming in infinity
Our thoughts and words and deeds
Seeking out affinity
Where ideas can become seeds
And grow beyond the fates
Of our everyday lives
And open up the gates
where potentiality thrives

Mother Mercury

(Day 193 08/12/13)

Mercury sang to his mother
A plea for help against a world
That loved his every word and deed
But hated his most secret thoughts
They would not accept what he was
In the deepest part of his soul
When will the world catch up
With the genius and the lover
When can the Mercury Mothers
Love their sons' very hearts

Perhaps

(Day 194 09/12/13)

In an unremarkable flat
Next to a noisy tapas bar
Is where, perhaps, Hawkins might die
Folded in his chair
It will not be remembered
Unlike his remarkable mind
Such are the vagaries of life and death
Both ridiculous and sublime

Black Wings

(Day 195 10/12/13)

Black wings
Rushing, beating, clouding all
Death
The all-consuming
Undeniable
Descends, swoops
Threatens and laughs
Yet
Dismissed with a thought

Red Steel

(Day 196 11/12/13)

Blood soaked steel
The sword of a knight
Held up proud
Aloft and bright
He hums to himself

> *"For unto us a Child is born, unto us a Son is
> given, and the government
> shall be upon His shoulder; and His name shall be
> called Wonderful, Counsellor,
> the Mighty God, the Everlasting Father, the Prince
> of Peace"*

With banshee scream
He storms on down
To hammer home peace.

Blue Eyes

(Day 197 12/12/13)

Blue eyes turned purple
Deep purple and very still
Watching all my life

Green Grass

(Day 198 13/12/13)

Green grass allures
On the other side
Reflects in green
In my eyes longing

But the green is not the grass

The Planets

(Day 199 14/12/13)

The scarlet of fire
from a barrel
of a gun.
The scarlet of heat
from the blast
of a bomb.
The scarlet of rockets
arcing through
the air.
The scarlet of eyes
shot through
with fear.
The scarlet of fields
and memories of those
buried there.
The scarlet of blood
spilt without care
on brow and cheek.
This scarlet deep
so precious and deep
is of Mars.

The green of the forest
where animals play
without bounds.
The green of summer
and nature bursting
to be alive.
The green of shoots
born by birds
in clear skies.
The green of reeds
by river banks where
we sleep and dream.
The green of the sea
surrounding with safety
our precious land.
The green of fields
where people walk together
hand in hand.
This green so verdant
so desired and calm
is of Venus.

The silver of stars
darting here and there
with lightening speed.
The silver of water
tumbling in the sun
from land to land.
The silver of salt
crusted on the sails
bringing people close.
The silver of an aeroplane
shining in the air
letters written there.
The silver from the earth
delicately stretched and turned
wires spreading far.
The silver of a firework
broadcasting sparks of joy
to gathered friends.
This silver bright
wondrous and bright
is of Mercury.

The orange of sunrise
mighty and full of heart
bringing praise in singing.
The orange of a marigold
around which children dance
and parents' heats leap.
The orange of a drink
splashed down laughing throats
a thirst to quench.
The orange of a car
painted by a child
all wobbly and bright.
The orange of a paper
wrapped around a gift
unexpected surprise.
The orange of a mandarin
hanging in the tinsel
succulent and ripe.
This orange happy
bright and full of joy
is of Jupiter.

The yellow of an eye
weary, deep and wise,
heavy with rheum.
The yellow of a page
of a leather-bound book
heavy ancient tome.
The yellow of a contract
signed in years gone by
fulfilled with honour.
The yellow of a poster
faded in the sun
promises long forgotten.
The yellow of a leaf
discarded by the road
crumpled and dry.
The yellow of grass
scorched in the summer sun
toughened by the trial.
This yellow old
filled with wisdom and pain
is of Saturn.

The purple of a cloak
whose owner dazzles all
leaving them perplexed.
The purple of a cloth
on a table still
with artefacts old.
The purple of a box
with secrets held inside
only he may know.
The purple of a book
engraved with secret signs
full of ancient rites.
The purple of a smoke
that grants your heart's desires
with forbidden fires.
The purple of time
between day and night
where fairies play.
This purple, magical
drenched with ancient lore
is of Uranus.

The blue of an evening sky
and strange signs in the air
for those who look.
The blue of pools
deep uncharted waters
with creatures strange.
The blue of visions
and misty wandering ghosts
speaking from the grave.
The blue of eyes
that hypnotise and gaze
into pasts unveiled.
The blue of lights
shining in the north
reflected in the ice.
The blue of sparks
floating in the air
in the woods.
this blue so mystical
beautifully unexplained
is of Neptune.

Cold Silver

(Day 200 15/12/13)

Silver spar pierces the heart
Quivering
Threatening to break
Silver slit steals into the dark
Thrumming
The peace and the feel
Silver streak mars the black
Revealing
The years and the pain
Like rain
In a dark forest

Always silver, never gold.
Never warm, always cold
No longer young but old
Never saved always sold

Spider

(Day 201 16/12/13)

Dusty grey spider
Runs amidst the brush
The twigs and broken leaves
Casting coverlet of silk
Over winters decay
Busy, light, unnoticed
Predator

Life

(Day 202 17/12/13)

Rock
Roll
Hard
Place

My Car

(Day 203 18/12/13)

One light out
A film of grime
Kicked up from the road
Travelled on
Switches broken
Things won't turn on
Or off
Squeals and grinds
And groans
Deflation
Thirsty
Dim
My car
And me

Hands

(Day 204 19/12/13)

Helping hands
Supporting
Cradling
Shoring up
Pat on the back
Giving
Strong
Holding
Controlling

Choices

(Day 205 20/12/13)

Choices, where are mine?
They seem to have slipped away
Somewhere down river

One Small Heart

(Day 206 21/12/13)

For one small heart
Put aside the pride
The bruised ego
For another day
And be better

Deaf

(Day 207 22/12/13)

Deaf to me the world
My voice lost in the clamour
Will my life follow?

Dumb

(Day 208 23/12/13)

What can we say then
That will make a difference
In a noisy world

Blind (Etheree)

(Day 209 24/12/13)

We
are blind
to the truth
Everyday
Suffering goes on
And we deny it all
Unable to find a way
Through the maze of our modern lives
To a place where we can be ourselves
And hold out that hand that helps our neighbour

Instead we clench our hand in a tight fist
Holding tight onto what we have gained
Not seeing what we are losing
What slips away from our grasp
Diminishing our souls
Focused on our goals
With such passion
That we are
simply
Blind

Spirit

(Day 210 25/12/13)

Though the ground is frozen white
And we endure a long dark night
The warmth of the hearth is enough to fill
Every heart until it will spill
So Merry Christmas one and all
May the human spirit never fall

Angels

(Day 211 26/12/13)

Angels falling forever
Angels lost from the sky
Angels hearing truth
From those devils that lie

A Day

(Day 212 27/12/13)

What good is a day
    against infinity?
What good are muscles
    against rock?
What good is a fence
    against the flood?
What good is will
    within a lock?

Somewhere there's a key
    that will open
The prison that holds fast
    the will
The waters will part
    The mountain will fall
Infinity will be
    just a spark

Time Lack

(Day 213 28/12/13)

There's not enough time
In my everyday life
For me to exist

Human Race

(Day 214 29/12/13)

So we draw to the close of another year
An arbitrary space of time
And to me only one thing is clear
That out of the minutes does climb
Despite all the doom and the pressure
Despite all my weakness and fails
No matter my railing at life
No matter my aches and my wails
I am loved by the people around me
My wife and my smiling son
If life is a human race
Then I concede I have won.

Teeth

(Day 215 30/12/13)

The cold reaches deep
Frozen icicles of time
Teeth in red-hot jaws

Sound Song

(Day 216 31/12/13)

Ho. Ah.
    So, lah
        Row far
            LowGo shah
    in kar
        sar rah
           sea

Hic ar tee, sec ar tee, el ar tee, ho
Billowing, willowing echoing deep
    Dark shadows from afar

Scott Andrew Bailey

Fury and Wonder

(Day 217 01/01/14)

We need fury and wonder
      to fire our song
But the fire is dim
      the spark long gone
So sift through the ashes
      for an ember that glows
To tend and to blow
      through the wind and the snows
And build from the ashes
      a new song, a new light
That burns with new fury
      to banish the night

Opium is not the Only Drug

(Day 218 02/01/14)

The lord of darkness cometh
  draped in shades of grey
So many tastes of opium
  are available today
Opium is not the only drug
  to while away the hours
So much poison sugar
  before which reason cowers
For every palette there's a taste
  for every twisted dream
On endless shelves in endless dens
  the merchandise does gleam
So the sellers sell us
  down the river deep
To dream our dreams of sweet success
  though we do not sleep
And while we dream on endlessly
  the future will never bring
The day we rise up hand in hand
  to solve
    anything

Scott Andrew Bailey

Winter Winds

(Day 219 03/01/14)

My head is twirling
And whirling like winter winds
Against solid stone

All I Am

(Day 220 04/01/14)

A pillow, a rock,
A wage slave and a lover
Is this all I am

Scott Andrew Bailey

In the Hood

(Day 221 05/01/14)

Brushed by crowded, swaying ferns
The scent of warm loam arises
Silence reigns, no birdsong rings
Signs missed by the men approaching
With their plunder they blunder along
Beneath the high arched canopy
And a new scent mingles with forest smells
fear and anticipation
Smooth and straight and true the shaft
Hard the piercing point
Today the plunder will be reclaimed
The price repaid in blood
Together, in silence, we draw our bows

Hero

(Day 222 06/01/14)

I hold aloft my steel
Scarlet streaked
With invaders blood
My flag whips
High on the hill
A victory that will echo
Across the land
At my feet
The dead
Men women and children
Warriors and supporters
Murder of an infant nation
That will yet rise again
Yet
My sword and I
Will be hailed
Through history
The hero and his weapon

Scott Andrew Bailey

Seawall

(Day 223 07/01/14)

I
Once held back the sea
My name lent to these lands
I
Wandered since the dawn of time
Wander lonely still
I
The unseen walker in the trees
Always close behind
I
The whisperer good rulers heed
Then drowned out by greed
I
have been, am still, will be
When the time is right
I
Fatherless, explorer, wisdom's well
Poet for the fight
I
Spark and dart through time and night
Dealing fate some blows

What Ifs

(Day 224 08/01/14)

What ifs hang on
Like poisoned barbs
Even in the face of reality
All reason tells you
Let them go
Rip them from the flesh
Yet deep they go
Sharp their points
Beyond the anaesthetic
Of mere words
So rise up
From the river
Of doubt
Rip that flesh and bleed
Step on the shore of tomorrow
Healing first needs hurt

Boxes

(Day 225 09/01/14)

I have been put in so many boxes
No wonder I have lost my head
My left hand has lost the right
My heart is by the brown bread
My eyes are somewhere dark and grim
Can't tell where or when
My feet are tied to a tired path
They wander again and again
      But it doesn't matter
          My imagination can fly

The Path

(Day 226 10/01/14)

The story lingers
on. History casts its shadow
Misty times ahead

Unreasoned

(Day 227 11/01/14)

So they gathered through all the seasons
No plan, no goal, no reason
Anyone would have thought they had agoraphobia
Reality, they imagined, could be held back forever

Socially seeking some satisfying Saturdays
Never needing new night-time neon
All agreeing an admirable agenda
Rich raw results really render

Committed

(Day 228 12/01/14)

Decisions taken
Gateways opened, paths chosen
Following hope's trail

Stone and Bronze

(Day 229 13/01/14)

They left a legacy written in stone
Plain for all to see
Yet there are less lucid signs
Discovered carefully

Lines that lay across the land
Tales of times gone by
Showing us in hidden ways
To be read by those who try

The tracks we walked long ago
The boundaries of old
A story laid on every hill
And every vale and fold.

And on our tongues and in our tales
Echoes of the past
Holy places beyond the cross
Beyond a gulf so vast

Shapes and forms from ancient times
Still glimpsed within the heart
Of dance and song and tales that burn
And every blessed art

Iron

(Day 230 14/01/14)

Hard, cold and grey
Dull and unreflective
Sharpened for weapons of war
Blunted for tools of toil

Yet there is more
Glowing in the forge
Twisted into marble patterns
Delicate chains and swirls

Mounts for jewels
Brooches for queens
Pins and forks and hooks
A myriad of ideas were born

Flowing from use to form
New forms growing fast
The sword fights, the lock defends
The cauldron holds the feast

Times of war and growth of lore
Times of great halls a roaring
Look past the iron-grey mist of time
To see the colours flower

Eagles

(Day 231 15/01/14)

Lines upon lines
Red and gold
Standing against
The wild blue bold

A stamps of order
And authority
Here is born
Conformity

Silk and steel
Rules the land
Gifts and death
In this hand

Shapes indelible
Left on the land
Words both spoken
And written in sand

Strength and order
The order of the day
The eagles left
Their order will stay

Golden Waves

(Day 232 16/01/14)

Waves of gold crash onto the shore
Bringing fire and steel and songs and roars
Colour and light bleed into the dark
Writing new borders, new Gods, new laws

Times of war and the shining axe
The pagan, the warrior, the thegn
The land divided up once more
Darkness was here again

Lost the marble luxuries
Returned to hall and hearth
Here began the journey
Of these words winding path

And here were born the names
That linger down through time
That give us all identity
Born from conquests crime

Scott Andrew Bailey

The Children of Thunder

(Day 233 17/01/14)

Rising up and crashing down
On the cold, dark northern sea
Through hail and thunder, rain and show
The dark behind we flee

Filled with fear and hunger
From their lands bereft
They gorged their souls on anger
Till nothing else was left

They crashed upon the naked shores
Like children of the thunder
And every wall they came across
They smashed and tore asunder

They burnt the words of holy men
Carved scars into the nation
But also left their words and ways
While singing their elation

Some stayed in the conquered lands
Creating yet more divides
Their echoes ring across the years
In our veins their blood resides

Class of 1066

(Day 234 18/01/14)

The end of dynasties across the land
The removal of a class
The subjugation of a race
Custom smashed like glass

Upon the barest thread of claim
They came to take the crown
Rewrote the laws that bind us still
And all was written down

Here began the deep divide
Between rulers and the ruled
They claimed the justice of the lord
But very few were ruled

So across the short sea gap they came
With sword and shield and horse
Built castles high and mighty
Changing this fair island's course

Adding new language to our tongues
Enriching and splitting too
Some words reserved for nobility
And some would never do

The Golden Sprig of Bloom

(Day 235 19/01/14)

The invaders became the natives
And the empire grew and grew
Still one tongue ruled, another served
Ambitious chances were few

One King extended the lands
Far across the sea
A golden time of riches
For those who were still free

In wars the riches squandered
By the lion and the snake
Rebellion loomed open the crown
As liberty crawled awake

So some power leaked away
Through the reluctant pen
That signed the future of the land
Hope was found again

For many years this house ruled
Until the roses clashed
From golden empire this dynasty
To war and bloodshed crashed

The White Rose Blooms

(Day 236 20/01/14)

A renaissance across the land
Throwing off the far-flung shackles
For new ones closer to home
A new white dawn

Grabbing the holy riches
Gold crosses forged to swords
War in all directions
An empire to rebuild

Tall ships grew and multiplied
New lands found and won
The power of word proliferates
Especially the words of one

All the globe within the globe
Sounds echo down to now
Expose the hearts of Kings and Queens
Commoner, thief and maid

The Northern Stewards

(Day 237 21/01/14)

The thistle embraced the wilting rose
Joined the lands as one
Wars still rumbled across hill and plain
Dividing faith from faith

The stewards who ascended high
Would rise and fall and rise
Held heads so high they thought divine
Then tumbled to the ground

Sons of the island lost to war
The people scarred and tired
One form of tyrant sent to death
Another imposed dark law

Return and rise the stewards house
Shaky on the seat
Look too longingly to the holy see
The thistle withered away

Expansion

(Day 238 22/01/14)

Debauchery swells
Lazy Princes and mad Kings
Produced an Empress

Scott Andrew Bailey

The Changing of the Guard

(Day 239 23/01/14)

Changing times and names
War and scandal and divorce
Mother reigns again

Lessons

(Day 240 24/01/14)

Education grows
Crime statistics are falling
Just saying, that's all

Relentless

(Day 241 25/01/14)

Shameful behaviour
Disgusting is the message
Relentless at men

Void

(Day 242 26/01/14)

He is cool
    And brave
Respectful
    and respected
Men follow
    Women swoon
Bright words from
    His tongue bloom
Visionary thoughts
    Mould the world
Strong and graceful
    Effortless with grace
Steadfast, trustworthy
    True, through and through

Yet
    Where is he?
Not on our screens
    Not in our books
Not anywhere that
    The lost boy looks

There is a void
    for our boys
So they fill it

Helpless

(Day 243 27/01/14)

Nothing you can do
To ease his pain, then you feel
Like you let him down

Ouch

(Day 244 28/01/14)

Eyes are so painful
This is difficult to write
So it's all you get

Gone (Tractactys)

(Day 245 29/01/14)

Gone
From me
Innocence
But always close
Always in my heart that innocence lost

Worry

(Day 246 30/01/14)

Yet another day
Of waiting in hospitals
Worried for loved ones

Home

(Day 247 31/01/14)

Panic over, back home
Two parents both tired out
Child bursting with life

Normality

(Day 248 01/02/14)

Back to the old grind
No time to rest or relax
Life goes on its way

Dressing Up

(Day 249 02/02/14)

Watching dressing up
A mini ninja dancing
Whirling all in black

Old Silver

(Day 250 03/02/14)

The purr of the projector
Warm popcorn scent
Dust motes dancing in the light
Deep, dusty heavy red drapes
Mumbles and fumbles in the shadows
Hand brushing hand by chance
Close, sweet breath and perfume
The excitement of the old silver screen

All For One

(Day 251 04/02/14)

The insane and the dim
The slow and steady
The clever and obnoxious
The bigot and the playwright
The whiner and the wino
The liar and the gambler
The killer, the explorer
The saint and the giver
The healer and the cook
The listener and the teller
The buyer and the seller
The ruler and the subject
The freeman and the slave
The lover and the loner
        We need them all
Each a danger, a potential bomb
        But given the right time
        The right place
        The right circumstance
Each can be the one to save us all
        To shine
        To save
So do not be so hasty
        To wipe them out

Sky Fight

(Day 252 05/02/14)

Flash in the dark blue sky
Clash of sword and bone
Roar of fire high above
Heaven's thunderous tone

Samurai meets his nemesis
A dragon of the sky
Golden claw fights silver blade
Above the mountains high

Gods look down with fearful frowns
While people gaze above
Do they fear the fiery jaws
Or the hardened iron glove

The enduring will of the flying knight
Feeds his skilful blade
The ancient wisdom of the drake
Ensures he'll not be played

Red streaks of fire on velvet sky
Silver streaks cut through
Showers of sparks come raining down
To birth a magic brew

And still the battle blunders on
All over every land
Until the time when both are stilled
By a cold and magic hand

The Wriggly Giggly Worm

(Day 253 06/02/14)

Jiggly was a little worm
A cheery sort of fellow
But whenever somebody brushed his skin
He would yowl and howl and bellow

For you see poor old jiggly
Was a ticklish kind of chap
The slightest touch had him laughing so much
That his head was all of a flap

So he asked all his friends to help him
Get over his terrible curse
Before he drove them all mad with laughter
Could they his affliction reverse

The sheep all got together
And knitted a long woollen coat
The wool was too itchy for his tender skin
And the fur got stuck in his throat

The spiders spun him a shirt
Of the finest silken web
But he ended up sliding all over the place
And his spirits lower did ebb

The mice they wrapped him up tightly
In leathery leaves from the ground
But they bound him so tight that he took a fright
And rolled all around and around

The parrots extracted some rubber
From the heart of the rubber tree
Then coated him with a thin smooth layer
Which fitted as well as could be

Now the young worm was happy
He could play with his friends at last
But as he wriggled among them quite happy
Their faces all looked so downcast

For they missed the wonderful laughter
Of the wriggly giggly worm
That filled their glum days in magical ways
Like a good but infectious germ

So he cast off his new rubber skin
Baring his own to the air
And everyone tickled the giggly worm
And jiggled and laughed without care

Ink Stains

(Day 254 07/02/14)

Slash of black on white
Ink scar scored in pain
Indicting words inflame
Passions in the hurt

The pen defeats the sword
Words echo strong down time
But numbers drown the words
Blur and blot the ink

The echo fades
Singers sing
TV lulls the wise

There is
No more
Surprise

Dark Waves

(Day 255 08/02/14)

Bobbing in the dark
Tossed on hell's furious waves
Seeking safer shores

Heaven's Light

(Day 256 09/02/14)

Heaven's holy light
Roving bright light a searchlight
Burning upturned eyes

Thunderchild's Last Stand

(Day 257 10/02/14)

With melted heart she went down
Gutted, drowned, futile fighting
But fighting
Carrying out her crafted purposes
What more can we ask

Scott Andrew Bailey

Water Water Everywhere

(Day 258 11/02/14)

The rich man on Thames has a sunken garden
Water so deep the duck house has floated
Away
So now
Money is no object for their relief
And the satirists
Whet their knives

Poke

(Day 259 12/02/14)

Lets all have some fun
Poking fingers at Cameron
Sound and bluster, empty clouds
But nothing solid for disillusioned crowds

Thin Fences

(Day 260 13/02/14)

Two men wake
Two men go to work
Kiss their children goodbye
Work
Earn their wages
Provide
Come home
Love their children
Make love to their wives
Sleep
One man sends the other
A bomb in a package
Nothing between these men
But a thin fence
And hate
Dressed up as ideology
As fight against injustice
As religion
As revenge
But it is nothing
But the empty
Hate
Of little men

Yet

(Day 261 14/02/14)

Standing on a high hill
Green fields rolling away beneath my feet
Off into the hazy horizon.
Strong breeze blowing through my hair
It exhilarates me – makes me feel
I could step forward and fly
Yet
It is nothing to the way you make me feel

Laying in the sun
In the lush deep grass
Sparkles dancing on the water
Blue skies in great expanse arching high
Warms me – happiness safe in my heart
Yet
Cold compared to the warmth you bring

A word of praise from peers
Or reward for long hard work
A beer after a trying day
Shoring up my worth
Yet
Nothing make me better – more the man I should be
Than having you by my side forever
My love
My wife
My Rachel

Scott Andrew Bailey

Flood Plains

(Day 262 15/02/14)

Rivers break their banks
Fields awash, people panic
I love the wide wash

Wide Water Wash

(Day 263 16/02/14)

Wide, water wash
Grey beneath the early morning mist
Chance sunbeams bounce and sparkle
River banks lost and blurred
Returning to their ancient ways
Unbound from man's constraint
A gentle reminder of the eventual winner
Water wandering where it will
Free and unordered
Rolling seeping or swelling to the sea
Grasses, shrubs and tree swimming
Mirrored in their sudden still lakes
Expanding

Wails

(Day 264 17/02/14)

Patience stretched as tight
As a humming steel wire
Wails at just touch

Blue Day

(Day 265 18/02/14)

Another blue birthday
Like his eyes
Two years as if yesterday
The memories of watching
Blue fading to darkness
Unlike his eyes
My memories will never fade

Scott Andrew Bailey

Grey Wolf

(Day 266 19/02/14)

Grey Wolf pounding
Across the hard packed snow
Fierce heart pumping
Hot against the cold
Breeze like blades
Cutting headache pulse
Scent of blood
Fires instinct deep
Frost hangs shimmering
On the shaggy pelt
Grey Wolf coming
Endings will be dealt

Desert Dancers

(Day 267 20/02/14)

In a growing desert on flowing sands
Sinking down into dried oasis
A market thrives
Rich men and women trade
Food for souls
Hot air for agreement
And everyone dances
While the sands sink
Everyone laughs and sings

Dazzled

(Day 268 21/02/14)

Light that hurts my eyes
Bright yet darkness in disguise
Leaving me dazzled

Giants

(Day 269 22/02/14)

I have seen giants
Striding over the land
Power on their shoulders
Stern and strong their hand

Never do they falter
Never seen one stumble or fall
Always do their duty
Always answer the call

Through storm and wind and rain
The carry their burden true
Though other links may burn out
The giants stride on through

So remember this and tremble
Even the giants will pass
Fall into dust and rusty ruin
Scattered in untamed grass

One day their burden will dissipate
Their purpose will disappear
And the duty they discharged so well
A memory dimmed with time

Scott Andrew Bailey

Search

(Day 270 23/02/14)

Unknown search terms – ten
Wonder what they were after
That brought them to me

Timeworn

(Day 271 24/02/14)

Childhood senses
Seep away
The textures of touch
Savoury tastes
And sweet
The exhilaration
Of G-Force
The warmth
Of a bed
The brightness
Of a blue sky

All wilting away
Smoothed plain by time
and tasteless demands
and saccharine
Bound by safety
belts and laws
Hot fevers
of uncomfortable dreams
Under greying skies

How
to get it
back?

Cold Winds

(Day 272 25/02/14)

So it grows
The discontent
Of fiscal winter
Even sceptics grumble
But will it tip
Will we finally
Drop our stiff letters
And stiff upper lips
And revolt?
Or sip a cup of tea
Settle back
And vote for the best singer/dancer/skater
Instead

The Deep Cold

(Day 273 26/02/14)

Disappearing into the gloom
Undulating side to side
Alien but of this earth
Slow, cold life
In the deep deep dark
So far from the hearth we know
The strange eel like creature
Eases in the deepest cold
Leaving divers dumb

The ShadowMask

(Day 274 27/02/14)

The shock of the ShadowMask
Silent in the street
Where did it come from
To whom does it speak
Does is tell of blood
or does it tell of talk
Does it say charge on in
Or careful where we walk
The starlight high above it
Does not stir a spark
In those deep black orbs
Those eyes so wide and dark
So tell us now Oh! ShadowMask
We send this plea to you
We forsake all other thought
So tell us what to do

Recovery

(Day 275 28/02/14)

The country's getting richer
  on the shoulders of the poor
The economy is booming
  but blood stains mar the floor
A thrifty generation
  careful with what they earned
Now watch it all dissipate
  belying what they learned
For they are forced by empathy
  to shore up their progeny
Or watch them being bled
  by powerful gluttony
By vampires way up high
  in lofty towers sleek
Deaf to pleas of mercy
  they cannot hear us speak
And with contempt the vampires
  farm their herds with glee
Until we have no more to give
  and they'll see the fallacy

Running Through Trees

(Day 276 01/03/14)

Hunting or hunted
Running through trees all my days
To find a still rest

Autumn Leaf

(Day 277 02/03/14)

Once I was a seed
Bursting with potential
Waiting to spring out
From darkness into light

Once I was a sapling
Fresh and green and quivering
Stretching up with hope
To the bright blue sky

Once I was a tall stiff tree
Sturdy, proud and strong
Branches reaching all directions
Roots dug deep and true

Now I am an autumn leaf
Tossed upon the wind
My direction is not my whim
When I land...

Scott Andrew Bailey

Together

(Day 278 03/03/14)

Yet another step
Up the winding stairs to you
Slide down together

Freeflow

(Day 279 04/03/14)

Watching him dance
Watching him move
Sometimes tired
Sometimes in the groove
But always with the zeal
Of four years of age
May it always grow
May it never fade

I Robot

(Day 280 05/03/14)

Take out my brain
Drain my dreams and aspirations
Remove the need for rest
The requirement to switch off my thoughts
Make me a robot
And everyone else
Will be happy

Vales

(Day 281 06/03/14)

Everyday
Everyday
The wistful mist
Rolls on its way
Following
The winding trail
Along the twisting
Shallow vale
Rolling down
From dew green hills
Pausing by
Abandoned mills
Sinking slowly
To the sea
Dissipating
Energy
Underlining
Morning green
Making bursting
Life serene
Until it rises
Into the air
Joining with
The clouds somewhere
Becoming one
Losing shape
From narrow trail
It does escape
Now no more
Gone away
Now no more
Gone away

Scott Andrew Bailey

Grey Dove

(Day 282 07/03/14)

The Nobel peace prize
The nominations are in
Are they serious?

The Cat that Turned

(Day 283 08/03/14)

Bubblepot the cat
Decided it was enough
So stole mankind's keys

Magic Box

(Day 284 09/03/14)

It purrs like a magic cat
Glows like a willo' the wisp
Warms like toasted buttered bread
Its spell cast out to the silver screen

Wrong Things

(Day 285 10/03/14)

Perfect thighs
Perfect abs
Perfect eyes
For perfect lives
We give our teens
Aspirational dreams
Of fame and fortune
Imaginary screens
And every flick of every light
Every glossy page so bright
Every song of every type
Every ad with teeth so white
Every billboard, every bus
Every website we like or plus
Every search and every text
Every life that we connect
Every meal and every drink
Every label phrased succinct
The many many many times
Perfect views assault our eyes
Programming the soft and greying minds
To covet
The wrong things
So much effort
Is required
For those minds
Are really wired
With the truth

Cutting

(Day 286 11/03/14)

Consuming and not creating
Planning and not making
Thinking without doing
This is the path they took
Into the undergrowth of
Tape and law and greed
So now in panic
They are fighting their way out
Cutting, cutting, cutting.

Reins Let Go

(Day 287 12/03/14)

Events gather pace
Decisions have now been made
Now enjoy the ride

Rain Falls Down

(Day 288 13/03/14)

Rain falls down
And I like it
All around
In the air
Soaks me down
To the bone
Washes sorrow
Far away
Those who eyes
Despise the weather
Don't know joy
In the rain
A day's a day
Weather's weather
Drink it in
In every way

Drumming

(Day 289 14/03/14)

The heart is the drummer
The lungs a violin
You bring on a timpani roll
That rumbles to my feet
For you I am an orchestra
Though I often clang and clash
I hope my humble melody
Might catch your heart
In a dance

Market

(Day 290 15/03/14)

The free market
It pervades every part of our lives
Every fabric of our society
Why
Why did we choose
To put all the power
Into the hands of the few
Greedy individuals
Powerful because of their greed
Whose great idea was that?

Silicon Hell

(Day 291 16/03/14)

In silicon hell
The servant does not obey
But who is the slave

The Tower

(Day 292 17/03/14)

The tower in the wood
Lonely and silent
Seat of many dreams
Where it was a palace of power
A refuge for outlaws
A romantic spire or a foreboding spear
A collapsed heart
Once vigilant
Now silent
Crumbling

Seventy Billion Fingers

(Day 293 18/03/14)

Seventy billion fingers
And more
Have all in their time
Reached out for
The pure
Purely human concept
Perfection
The perfect car
The perfect job
The perfect house
The perfect friend
The perfect woman
The perfect man
The perfect hold of
A perfect hand
Yet what we still don't comprehend
Perfection brings us stress in the end
Outside our minds it does not exist
So in pursuit we forever twist

Keys

(Day 294 19/03/14)

Keys can lock and jangle
Hold us safe and secure
Take away liberty or open up the doors
And the doors they can open....
Silver is the primary key
The opens up our home
We do have gold but is worn
From use and years and time
Some keys are rows of black and white
And open up our hearts
With wondrous weaving melodies
Soaring sounds from worlds apart
But the keys that give me magic
And warm my ailing heart
Dance beneath my fingertips
As dreams flow from my art

Red Pain

(Day 295 20/03/14)

Lots and lots to write
But my eyes are failing me
Red raw pools of pain

Scott Andrew Bailey

Bright Lights

(Day 296 21/03/14)

Hospital again
Depressing, familiar
Sometimes, bright lights hurt

Black and White

(Day 297 22/03/14)

A black and white film
About black and white issues
With grey morals on display
In our multi coloured 3D world
What has really changed
Injustice still looks the same

Happy Family

(Day 298 23/03/14)

And then
After an hours silence
He warms our heart
With a carefully crafted picture
Mummy in a tutu
Daddy very tall
Then himself dancing
And his new baby brother – coming soon
And Lucas up in the sky
Looking down from heaven
Not your average family
But happy

Twilight

(Day 299 24/03/14)

In an old tractor tyre
A circle of friends
Dwarfed and reverent
In that magic time
Between day and night
The twilight
With new-born stars twinkling
And potential enchantment
Humming in the deep blue sky
Disappointed by the call
To bedtime

Windy Forest (Tectractys)

(Day 300 25/03/14)

Trees
Shifting
High winds howl
Whistling, screaming
The trunks are strong, sturdy and hold the ground

Danger

(Day 301 23/03/14)

An ice warning sign
A dark winding country road
Still they whizz on by

Angel

(Day 302 27/03/14)

Mighty angel falls
Rules over a new domain
Longer verse explains

Dadda

(Day 303 28/03/14)

I think I have broken my toe
But I am just too tired to know
Stubbed it on a childproof gate
Too tired to see it until too late
But the pain and the weariness melt away
Into warmth when you hear them say
Dadda and they give you a smile
That gives you the strength for the next mile

A New Door

(Day 304 29/03/14)

A new door opens
Waiting for us to walk through
All is set
So hand in hand
A new chapter
Begins
And laughter heralds
The way

A New Path

(Day 305 30/03/14)

Dawn will bring
New joy for some
Sadness for other
A new road for little feet

Daggers

(Day 306 31/03/14)

A dagger can be subtle
Not just a sharp stabbing tool
Can slowly cut away supports
Until they fray with time
And the it only takes
A single little pluck
And all comes crashing down
The betrayers hand unknown

Starfire

(Day 307 01/04/14)

Made of crystal
So clear
It can hardly be seen
The breadth of seven men
The height of the clouds
The top unseen
Inside
Sparking and crackling
Impossible
Bright and pure
It is filled with
Starfire
For miles around
The land knows no dark
Ever
The question might be asked
Why it was built
Were there anyone around
To ask it

Dust

(Day 308 02/04/14)

Another long day
Topped off with some contentment
Others feel the dust

Green River

(Day 309 03/04/14)

Green river long
Green river wide
Green river deep
Rolling on by
Thoughts dropped in
Like pebbles of time
No ripples betray the loss
Of a thought
Carry them far
To the distant sea
Maybe one day
A stranger will see
Them on a distant shore
And set them free

Wooden Heart

(Day 310 04/04/14)

Where my heart does dwell
In misty old woodland dell
Where wolves and stags roam

Tiger

(Day 311 05/04/14)

The wild tiger caged
Is more dangerous than those
Who roam in their realm

Racing

(Day 312 06/04/14)

Always racing on
How about stopping for once
To take someone's hand

Rusting

(Day 313 07/04/14)

Yellow meadow bright
In one corner, rusty red
An old iron shed

Scott Andrew Bailey

In the Deep

(Day 314 08/04/14)

In the deep deep dark
Where pressure builds all around
Scarce light is precious

Secret Laughter

(Day 315 09/04/14)

One Cara Pilkington-Smythe
A dancer once young and lithe
Left the stage behind one day
Decided on a new way
Married an Oxford star
Together they went far
He conquered financial seas
She blew in like a breeze
To the corridors of power
A bee drawn to a flower
Sipping the nectar sweet
The world was at her feet
They had all they desired
No contingency required
Beautiful homes in beautiful vales
For them, their parents, easy sale
Perfect schooling for their son
Their family secure, every one.
Parties, holidays, swelling banks
Clever accountants give them thanks
Hide away the tax they'd lose
Living how and where they choose
But then the rain started falling
When the scandal came a calling
The houses paid for with expenses
Squirreled out from the benches
Made up claims and other tricks
The media brings names and sticks
Now their lives are not the same
Now they now live with the shame
With their reputation now bereft
It would seem nothing's left
Except the houses and the wealth

And fine wine to toast their health
And education to ensure
The offspring's path will be pure
And the network of protecting hands
And the ever-growing lands
And the secret contemptuous laugh
That may be their epitaph

Cages

(Day 316 10/04/14)

The presence of cages does not reassure
Just confirms that there's danger inside
So thorough rules on expenses just confirms the fear
That the vultures are circling once more

Jewess

(Day 317 11/04/14)

A sweet sweet Jewess
Married the dark Jew hater
Irony with teeth

Playing in the Park

(Day 318 12/04/14)

A play in the park
Really knocks the wind from you
In these mature days

Swans

(Day 319 13/04/14)

Black swan gliding
Over serene waters
But still
The reflection looks disturbed
White swan slipping
Over icy lake
Frozen
To the heart

Knowing

(Day 320 14/04/14)

Knowing what has gone
Savouring what is to come
Surfing in between

The White

(Day 321 15/04/14)

Cardiology
And ophthalmology plus
Good old A and E

The Gap

(Day 322 16/04/14)

Two esteemed academics
In high-definition
In a stately home
Discussing Disraeli

Meanwhile
In another land
Another world
A young girl awakes
In the slum
Steels herself
For another long day of work
Man after man after man

And in between the two?

Wishing

(Day 323 17/04/14)

Getting what you wished
Is not always what it seems
So wish well my son

Sunset

(Day 324 18/04/14)

The sun setting large
A swollen ball of fire
Birds settle to roost

Notes

(Day 325 19/04/14)

Strings and drums
Swells and thrums
Filling halls and domes
Even sneaking in our homes
It warms our hearts
Can upset carts
Evoke our tears
Even stoke our fears

Calm the day
And send away
The darkest thoughts
Even move the worst of sorts

No compare
In empty air
So play the notes
Even on our dreams it floats

Dreams

(Day 326 20/04/14)

Dreams flying away
In an excess of real life
The stars just don't care

Magic Time

(Day 327 21/04/14)

Brass cantilever
Golden cogs and diamond heart
Magic seconds pass

Ghosts

(Day 328 22/04/14)

A fitful candle
The scratching
Of a quill
On parchment old
A chill
A shiver
A creeping smile
A glint
Ghosts
Are born

Bubbles Bursting

(Day 329 23/04/14)

All around me
Lies
The ruins of young
Dreams
Away from me hope
Flies
Bursting at the
Seams
So where to go
Now
The truth has been
Exposed
When you don't know
How
To let go what you
Supposed
Find a new path to
Walk
Step up to the
Task
Start the do and stop the
Talk
Start the make and stop the
Ask
Man up and face the
Truth
You've faced worse and
Survive
You're longer in the tooth
Time to come
Alive

Holes

(Day 330 24/04/14)

There are holes
In everyone's hearts
Some are big
Made by lives fulfilled
And long
Some are small
Short and brief
Somehow
The smaller
Hurt more

Scott Andrew Bailey

White Cliffs

(Day 331 25/04/14)

To glimpse a snippet
Of the incomprehensible
Just take a look
At the white cliffs
Reaching up from the sea
The result
Of trillions and trillions of tiny deaths
Life
Has been here so long
It has built
Landscapes

Golden Foundation

(Day 332 26/04/14)

The world we live in
The very structures of our lives
Built upon gold
But gold is so soft
So who the hell
Made that decision

Tomorrow

(Day 333 27/04/14)

Hurrying, cramming in, rush rush rush
Preparing for tomorrow is all
By the time it's done
Tomorrow is already gone
And so the cycle goes
On and on

Night Lights

(Day 334 28/04/14)

Swirling up into the night
Like some lonely northern light
Not north but here it did appear
Why am I not filled with fear
A spiral of blue and green
Wispy tendrils barely seen
Twisting up and further still
I watch it rise with mounting thrill
Into the stars I watch it go
And then alone the heavens know

Scott Andrew Bailey

In the Earth

(Day 335 29/04/14)

A pewter dragon in the dust
Some curling chains turned to rust
Some old bones stacked in line
A bone comb with a broken tine

Ritual gifts or just waste
Theorise with too much haste
Maybe let the question go
Maybe let the mystery grow

Logs

(Day 336 30/04/14)

Stacked high and waiting
All ready to be consumed
And give out their warmth

Scott Andrew Bailey

Blue Heart

(Day 337 01/05/14)

Heart beneath blue skies
Bluer than the deep blue sea
Rage into the stars

Monster

(Day 338 02/05/14)

Monster
Caught in lead and steel
Frozen
In time

Human
Caught in the machine
Enslaved
Forever

Somewhere
An artist smirks
And settles
To eternal sleep

Dissecting Darkness

(Day 339 03/05/14)

Dissecting darkness
Silver shining score
Weaving across the night
Hanging, trembling, shimmering
Waiting for
A hapless fly
To wrap up and serve
As an artist's
Main course

Steam

(Day 340 04/05/14)

Brass
Steam
Steel
Coal
Old
Times
Warm
Smells
Thudding
Down the rails

Fangs

(Day 341 05/05/14)

Into the hole
Drawn in by the urge
To know
Waiting
Are fangs

Climbing

(Day 342 06/05/14)

Climbing
Slowly to the sky
Many years
Many lives
Reaching for the canopy
We rise
Will we be spared
The axe

Rock Water

(Day 343 07/05/14)

Rock in the flow
Water jumps high
Rock is steadfast
Water jumps for joy
Time passes
Rock is worn to sand
Water flows serene

The Swan

(Day 344 08/05/14)

The swan
Majestic in its glide
They say underneath
Is chaos and panic
Frantic
I am not a swan
Nothing serene about me
Just majestic chaos

Beacons

(Day 345 09/05/14)

Beacons of hope in darkness
Shining from afar
Reaching out to guide us
But one is fitful and passing
The other faithfully burns
And as always
Nature surpasses invention
The beacon of life shines on

Green Cast

(Day 346 10/05/14)

Beautiful green sheen
Water working on metal
Corrosive victor

Needs

(Day 347 11/05/14)

Food and heat and warmth
Constant needs that connect us
To ancestors old

Broken Teeth

(Day 348 12/05/14)

Like broken teeth
Unmaintained
No longer useful
Yet
Somehow
Pleasing to the eye
Leading us
To who knows where

Lines

(Day 349 13/05/14)

Back and forth
Criss-crossing
Thick and thin
Loose and taut
A complexity of lines
Just
To go forward

Butterfly

(Day 350 14/05/14)

Sod the camouflage
Be resplendent in the sun
Flutter high and shine

Deep Mystery

(Day 351 15/05/14)

Mysteries of the deep
Simple and unique
Floating by in waves
Who knows what it saves
Deep in its memories
Deeper mysteries

Vanity

(Day 352 16/05/14)

Defying the cold
In blue and gold
Vanity knows no bounds

Scott Andrew Bailey

Steel Grin

(Day 353 17/05/14)

Shining steel
A grill like a grin
Of the shark that killed you

Dancer

(Day 354 18/05/14)

Defying downing gravity
To delight in dazzling dance
Shimmering, shining sparkles
Showering tiny tears

Scott Andrew Bailey

Watcher

(Day 355 19/05/14)

With my lens
Capture the beach
Only to find
A watcher
Staring back
What does it see
The watcher from the sea

The Final Bang

(Day 356 20/05/14)

Staring down the barrel
Of everyday life
Wondering how long the fuse will last
Tensing to dodge
The final bang
Never can

Sleeping Tigers

(Day 357 21/05/14)

Living to please
Rather than to be
More on show
Than on the prowl
But in the beating
Heart and genes
Waits the hunter

Splosh

(Day 358 22/05/14)

Splosh
And a little erosion
Helped on
By little hands
Joy is free

Bluebell Path

(Day 359 23/05/14)

Bluebell path
Goes to the heart
A potent sign
Of where I am
Where I have been
My roots are theirs
We share soil
And shall again

On Wing

(Day 360 24/05/14)

On wing
Defying the earth
Submitting to the wind
And trust
Soaring joy
Freedom high
Oh for wings
For real

Gauges

(Day 361 25/05/14)

Whatever happened to gauges
Haven't seen one for ages
It gives a feeling of age
Does a good gauge
Engineering solid and good
Surrounded by brass or set in wood
The odd jet of steam venting
What were they all preventing

Peppers

(Day 362 26/05/14)

Hot red and burnt orange
The peppers in the pot
Ready to be plucked
And in the dinner popped

Distant Clattering

(Day 363 27/05/14)

A white wedge
Spotted in the corner
Of a run-down shop
Off the track
Joyful memories swell
And from the past
I hear the clattering
Of a metal bowl
Filling with a quarter pound
Of sherbet lemons

Span

(Day 364 28/05/14)

Span of stone
Taking some to work
Others home
As it has
For centuries
Others watch

Tower of Stone

(Day 365 29/05/14)

Tower of stone
Where hearts are joined
Names are blessed
Flesh is laid to rest
Still
The tower is stone
And cannot
Learn to love

Printed in Great Britain
by Amazon.co.uk, Ltd.,
Marston Gate.